NATIONAL GEOGRAPHIC
KiDS

Sun

Stephen M. Tomecek
Illustrated by Carla Golembe

NATIONAL GEOGRAPHIC
WASHINGTON, D.C.

To Phil and Jane and all the people in Learning Technologies who helped put the stars in my eyes!
—ST

For Harriet Finkelstein and for Barbara Solomon. You shine!
—CG

It happens every morning.
You jump out of bed, and as you wipe the sleep
from your eyes, you see it. The sun rises in the sky
and a new day begins. Even on cloudy days
the sun gives us light.

4

What is the sun?
Why is it so bright?

What makes it rise and set and move across the sky?
How big is the sun, and how far is it from Earth?

To find the answers, just follow the sun.

The sun is a star. It's our star!
When most people think about stars,
they imagine those tiny points of light that
can be seen only in the night sky.

The reason our sun seems so big
and bright and other stars look like little dots is
that all the other stars are much farther away.
The sun is the closest star to Earth. If you could travel
far into space and get close to other stars,
they would look as big as our sun does.

Even though the sun is our closest star, it's still very far away from Earth. The sun is about 93 million miles from Earth. If you had to drive 93 million miles at 60 miles per hour, it would take you almost 177 years. And that's without stopping to eat a snack.

Because the sun is so far away from Earth, it doesn't look that big, but it's really gigantic.

If you could measure the sun across its center, you would find that it is about 865 thousand miles across. That means that you could put 109 Earths across the face of the sun!

The sun is not made of rock, as our Earth is.
It is made mostly of two hot gases called hydrogen
and helium. Helium gas is what makes balloons float.
It is lighter than air. Hydrogen gas is also light,
and if you bring hydrogen near a fire, it explodes.

Even though it may look as if it
is on fire, the sun is not burning.
Explosions similar to nuclear bombs
make the gases hot. The surface
of the sun is more than
11 thousand degrees Fahrenheit
(6 thousand degrees Celsius).
If Earth were any closer to
the sun, it would be too hot
for us to live here.

Because the sun is so bright,
you should never look right at it.
Even if you are wearing sunglasses, you can hurt your
eyes if you look at the sun for only a few seconds.

When scientists study the sun, they don't usually look at it directly. First, they put special filters on their telescopes, and then they use cameras to take pictures of the sun. What they have found is that the surface of the sun is constantly changing.

The sun is covered with dark and
light patches. Scientists call the dark patches
sunspots. They think that sunspots are a kind
of giant storm. Sunspots look dark because they
are cooler than the rest of the surface of the sun.
The number of sunspots changes all the time.

Sometimes the sun shoots large
bursts of hot gas out into space.
Scientists call these bursts solar flares.

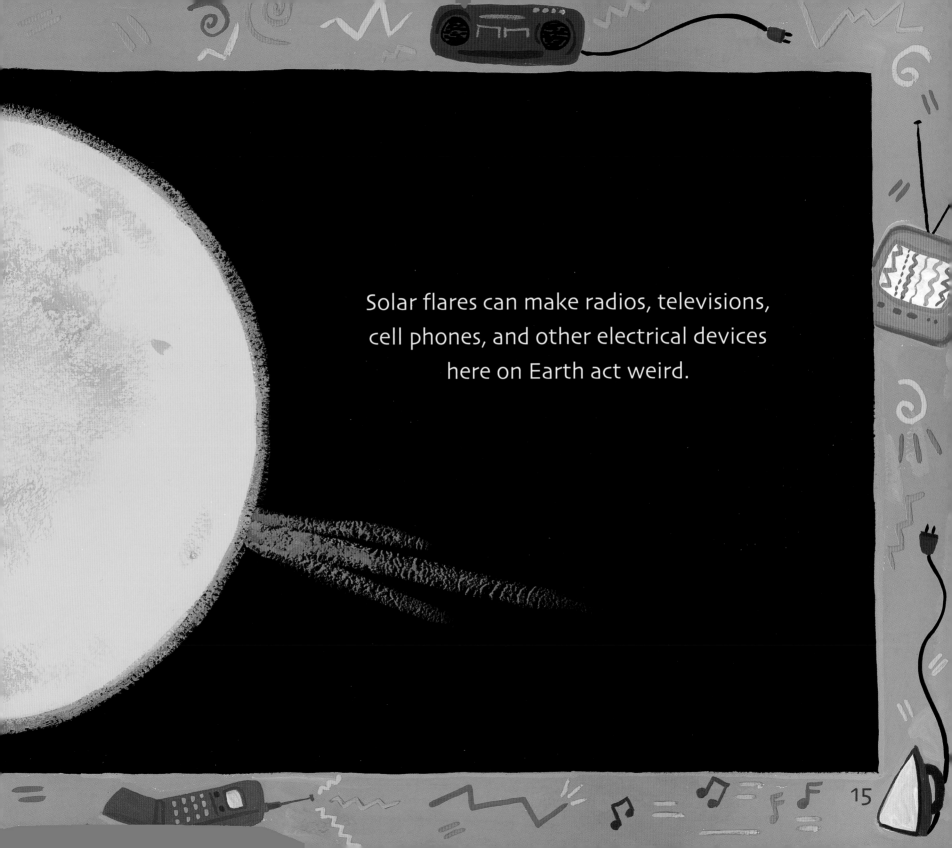

Solar flares can make radios, televisions,
cell phones, and other electrical devices
here on Earth act weird.

Have you seen how the sun seems to move across the sky? The sun seems to rise in the east and set in the west.

Many years ago, people thought that
the sun traveled around Earth. They thought that
Earth was the center of everything.

Today we know that it's really Earth that is moving,
not the sun. Even though we can't feel it, Earth is always
spinning, just like a basketball on a player's finger.
The line that Earth spins around is called an axis.

Because Earth is spinning on its axis like a big ball, sometimes you are on the side that faces the sun, and sometimes you are on the side that faces away from the sun. When you're on the side that faces the sun, the sun's light shines on you. That's daytime.

When the place you are on turns away from the sun, it gets dark. That's night. It takes Earth about 24 hours to make one complete spin. That's a day.

JANUARY
31 days

FEBRUARY
28 days

MARCH
31 days

APRIL
30 days

MAY
31 days

JUNE
30 days

JULY
31 days

AUGUST
31 days

SEPTEMBE
30 days

OCTOBER
31 days

NOVEMBE
30 days

DECEMBE
31 days

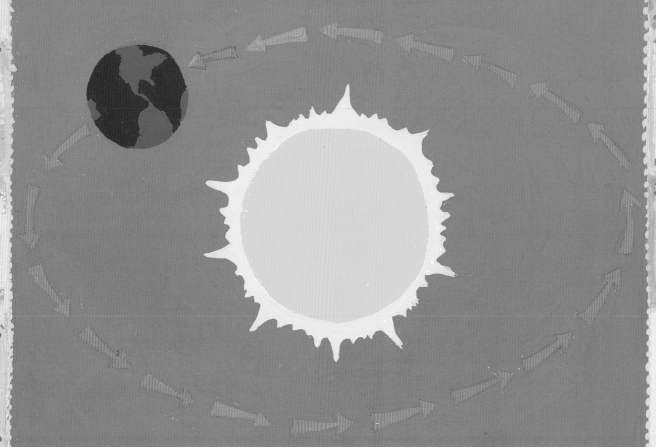

Besides spinning, our Earth is also moving around
the sun in a slightly oval-shaped path called an orbit.
It takes about 365 days—one year—for the Earth
to make one trip, or orbit, around the sun.
How many orbits old are you?

The axis of the Earth is tilted a bit.
As our Earth orbits the sun, sometimes the
place where you are is tilted toward the sun,

TOWARD

AWAY

and sometimes the place where you are is tilted away
from the sun. This is why the Earth has seasons.
If the Earth weren't tilted in its orbit,
the season would always be the same!

During the summer, the sun appears to be high overhead in the sky. If you watch the clock, you'll see that there are more hours of daylight in the summer than in any other season. Summer is warm because the part of the Earth you are on is tilted toward the sun.

During the winter, the sun appears to be closer to the horizon. The horizon is where the sky and the ground meet. There are fewer hours of daylight and it's colder in the winter because the part of the Earth you are on is tilted away from the sun.

Our Earth isn't the only planet that
goes around the sun. Seven other planets do too.
In order out from the sun the planets are
Mercury, Venus, Earth, Mars, Jupiter, Saturn,
Uranus, and Neptune.

The sun is the center of our neighborhood in space.
We call our neighborhood the solar system.
Can you match each planet with its name?

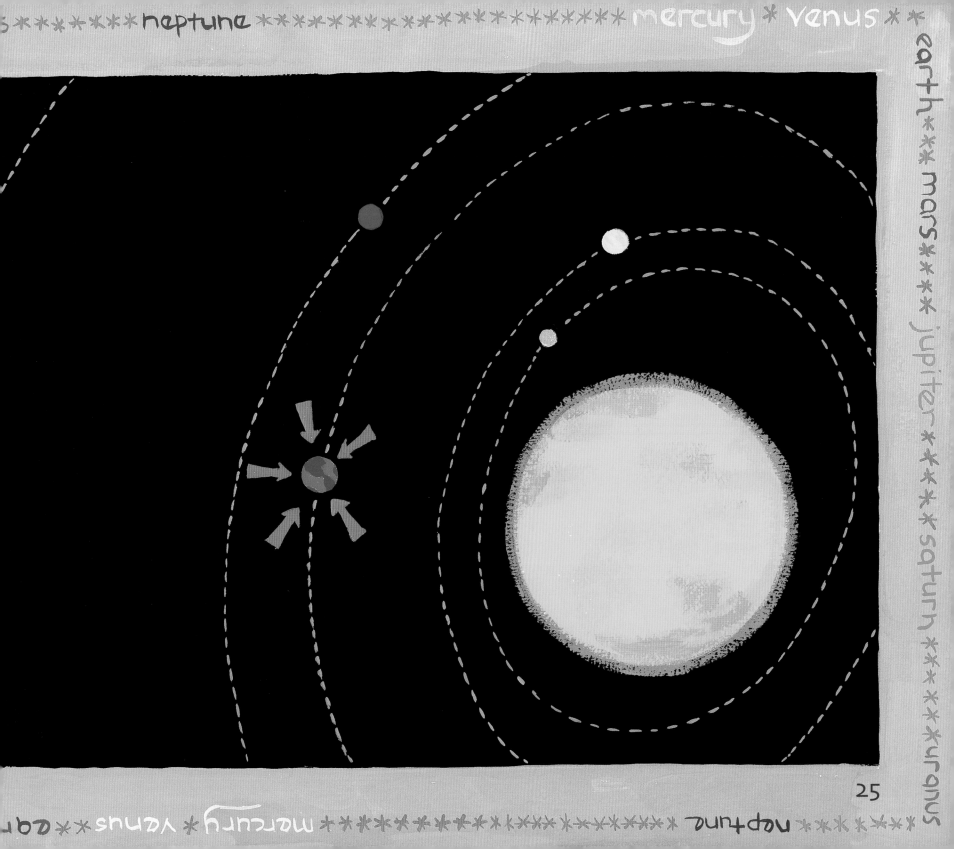

Without the sun, most things would not
be able to live here on Earth. Without sunlight,
plants could not grow. Without plants, people
and other animals would have no food.

The sun also keeps Earth warm.
When sunlight hits the rocks and water on Earth's surface,
some of the light is soaked up and turned into heat.

Without this heat from the sun,
all of the water on Earth would freeze.

Our sun is truly special.
It gives us light. It gives us life.
The sun is the biggest thing in our solar system.
You might even say that it's our "star" attraction.

What Time Is It?

If you'd like to see how the sun makes day and night here on Earth, you can make your own model.

Here's what you'll need:

* A large ball, such as a basketball
* A flashlight
* A small piece of paper
* A pencil
* Scissors
* Sticky tape
* A friend

1. Draw a small picture of yourself on the paper.

2. Tape the picture to the ball.

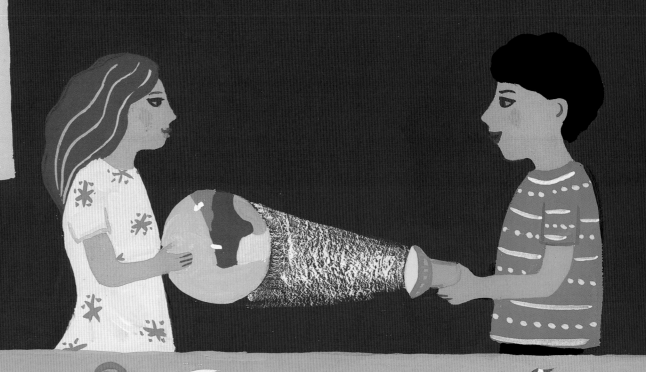

3. Make the room dark.

4. Hold the ball in your hands. Have your friend or a grown-up point the flashlight at the ball from a foot away.

5. Turn the ball slowly.

What happens to your picture as the ball turns?

How does the model explain day and night on Earth?

What Did You Discover?

Use a mirror to read!

In this experiment, the ball is Earth and the flashlight is the sun. As the ball turns, the picture is first in light and then in dark. When the picture is in light, it's daytime. When the picture is in dark, it's night.

Jump Into Science series consultant: Gary Brockman,
Early Education Science Consultant

To create her paintings, Carla Golembe used gouache on watercolor paper.

The solar system drawing on pages 24-25 is not to scale.
The text type used in this book is set in Skia. The title type is set
in GreyMantle and has been altered by the designer.

Book design by Sharon Davis Thorpe, Panache Designs

The Library of Congress cataloged the 2001 edition as follows:
Sun / by Stephen M. Tomecek ; illustrated by Carla Golembe.
p.cm.—(Jump into Science)
Summary: Introduces sunspots and solar flares and how the sun creates
night and day, and seasons, how the sun warms the planet Earth, and more.
ISBN 978-0-7922-8200-6 (hard cover)
I. Sun—Juvenile literature. [1. Sun] 1. Golembe, Carla,
ill. II. Title. Series.
QB521.5. T66 2001
2000012759

2016 paperback edition ISBN: 978-1-4263-2368-3
2016 reinforced library binding ISBN: 978-1-4263-2369-0

Steve Tomecek
is the Executive Director and founder of
Science Plus, Inc. He is the author of three
other Jump Into Science books as well as
several other titles, including the winner
of the 1996 American Institute of Physics
Excellence in Science Writing Award. He
lives in Bellerose, New York.

Carla Golembe
is the author/illustrator of a number of
books for children, including *Dog Magic,
Annabelle's Big Move,* and *M Is for Maryland.*
She has received illustration awards from
the *New York Times,* Parents' Choice, and
the American Folklore Society. She lives in
Silver Spring, Maryland, with her husband
and two cats of normal colors.

Since 1888, the National Geographic Society has funded more than 12,000 research,
exploration, and preservation projects around the world. The Society receives funds from
National Geographic Partners, LLC, funded in part by your purchase. A portion of the pro-
ceeds from this book supports this vital work. To learn more, visit www.natgeo.com/info.

For more information, visit www.nationalgeographic.com,
call 1-800-647-5463, or write to the following address:

NATIONAL GEOGRAPHIC PARTNERS, LLC
1145 17th Street N.W.
Washington, D.C. 20036-4688 U.S.A.

National Geographic supports K-12 educators with ELA Common Core Resources.
Visit natgeoed.org/commoncore for more information.

Printed in China
16/PPS/1

EDUCATIONAL EXTENSIONS

1. Based on the reading, why does the sun look
   so much larger than the stars we see at night
   even though it is not the largest star?

2. Give an oral report on how your life would be
   different if there was no sun in the sky. What
   could you do or not do?